CAMBRIDGE
Primary Science

Workbook 5

Fiona Baxter & Liz Dilley

CAMBRIDGE
UNIVERSITY PRESS

University Printing House, Cambridge CB2 8BS, United Kingdom

One Liberty Plaza, 20th Floor, New York, NY 10006, USA

477 Williamstown Road, Port Melbourne, VIC 3207, Australia

314–321, 3rd Floor, Plot 3, Splendor Forum, Jasola District Centre, New Delhi – 110025, India

79 Anson Road, #06–04/06, Singapore 079906

Cambridge University Press is part of the University of Cambridge.

It furthers the University's mission by disseminating knowledge in the pursuit of education, learning and research at the highest international levels of excellence.

www.cambridge.org
Information on this title: www.cambridge.org/9781108742962

© Cambridge University Press 2021

First published 2014

Second edition 2021

20 19 18 17 16 15 14 13 12 11 10 9 8 7 6 5 4 3 2 1

Printed in Malaysia by Vivar Printing

A catalogue record for this publication is available from the British Library

ISBN 978-1-108-74296-2 Paperback with Digital Access (1 Year)

Contents

Contents

How to use this book

This Workbook provides questions for you to practise what you have learned in class. There is a unit to match each unit in your Learner's Book. Each topic is divided into three parts:

Focus: these questions help you to master the basics. ⟶

Focus

1 Match each word about how seeds grow with its description.
Draw a line from the word to its meaning.

Word	Description
Germination	The first part that grows
Water	Grows upwards
First root	When a seed starts to grow
First shoot	Makes the seed swell

Practice: these questions help you to become more confident in using what you have learned. ⟶

Practice

3 Identify and colour in the different parts of the flower.

Use these colours:

- green – sepals
- blue – petals
- orange – anther
- black – filament
- yellow – stigma
- brown – ovary

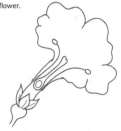

Challenge: these questions will make you think very hard. ⟶

Challenge

Look at the drawing of a flower.

5 Write labels on the drawing for parts A, B, C and D.

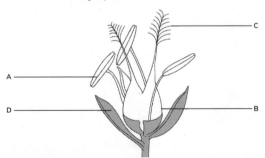

1 Life cycles of flowering plants

> 1.1 Flowering and non-flowering plants

Focus

1   Look at the pictures of plants. Which plants are flowering plants and which plants are non-flowering plants? Write 'flowering' or 'non-flowering' in the space below each picture.

A _____

B _____

C _____

D _____

E _____

F _____

2   The diagram shows the life cycle of a flowering plant.

Use the words in the box to help you label the diagram.

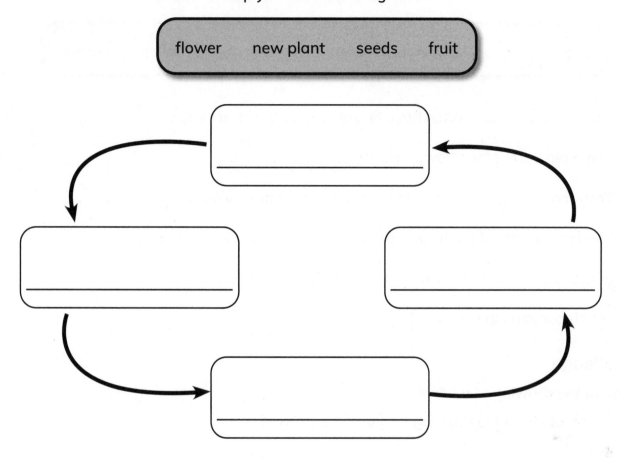

flower   new plant   seeds   fruit

Practice

3   Identify and colour in the different parts of the flower.

Use these colours:

- green – sepals
- blue – petals
- orange – anther
- black – filament
- yellow – stigma
- brown – ovary

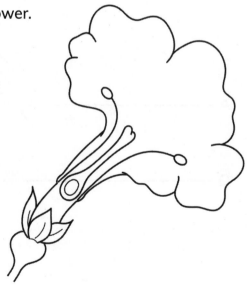

4 These sentences describe the different parts of a flower and their functions.

Use the words in the box to fill in the spaces below.

stigma   ovary   petals   anthers   stamens   pollen   carpel

The _____ often have bright colours to attract insects.

The male parts of the flower are the _____.

They make _____ in their tips, which are called _____.

The female part of the flower is the _____. It is made up

of the _____, which collects pollen, and the _____,

which contains the eggs.

Challenge

Look at the drawing of a flower.

5 Write labels on the drawing for parts A, B, C and D.

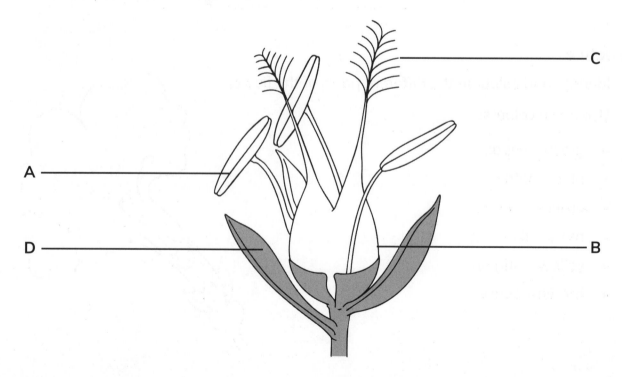

6 a Which part of the flower is missing?

_____

b Add the missing part to the drawing.

7 What colour would you expect the following parts to be? Explain your answers.

a Part A

_____

_____

b Part D

_____

_____

> 1.2 Pollination, fruits and seeds

Focus

1 Use the words in the box to complete the sentences about pollination and fruit and seed formation. You will use some words more than once.

> wind   insects   seeds   eggs   pollen   stigma
>
> anthers   nectar   ovary   fertilisation

a The _____ of flowers make a yellow powder. This is called _____ .

b Pollination happens when pollen moves from the _____ to the

_____ of a flower of the same type.

c Some plants use _____ to blow the pollen far away.

d _____ visit flowers to feed on _____ . They get _____
on their bodies at the same time.

e The pollen and the _____ join together. This happens inside the

_____ during _____ . This is how _____ form.

f The _____ becomes the fruit.

Practice

Aliyah's class investigated a scientific question. These are their results.

Colour of flower	Number of insects that visited flower
Red	3
Yellow	12
White	10
Blue	6

2   a   Suggest the question that Aliyah's class investigated.

_____

    b   Identify the type of scientific enquiry they used in their investigation.
        Choose from the following types: fair testing, research, observing over time,
        identifying and classifying, looking for patterns.

_____

3   Draw a bar chart of the results.

Flower colour

4   a   Which colour flower did the most insects visit?

_____

    b   Which colour flower did the fewest insects visit? Suggest a reason for your answer.

_____

_____

5   a   What conclusion can you make from these results?

_____

_____

b   What can you do to be sure your conclusion is correct?

_____

_____

Challenge

Some kinds of flowers have male parts or female parts only.
The flowers shown in the drawings only have male or female parts.

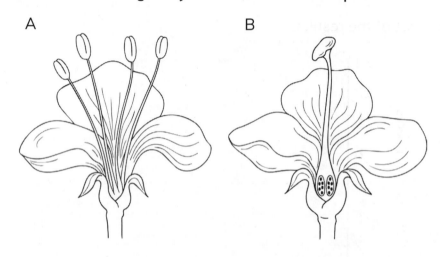

6   Which is the male flower and which is the female flower? Say how you know.

_____

_____

_____

7   Describe the process of pollination in flowers like these.

_____

_____

_____

_____

8   Draw arrows on the drawings to show how pollination happens.

› 1.3 How seeds are spread

Focus

1 What do we call the spreading of seeds away from the parent plant?

_____

2 How are these seeds spread? Sort them into groups and write the names
of the seeds in the table.

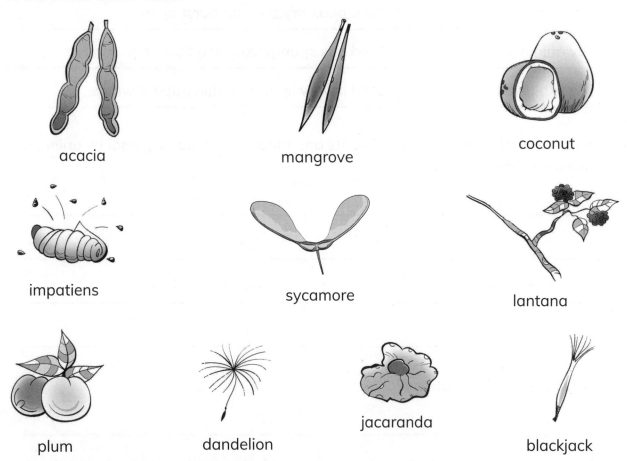

acacia

mangrove

coconut

impatiens

sycamore

lantana

plum

dandelion

jacaranda

blackjack

Eaten	Stick on	Fly away	Float	Explode

9 ›

Practice

3 Match the way seeds are spread in the first column with the description of how the seed or fruit is adapted to the way it is spread in the second column.
Draw a line from the way the seed is spread to the description of the seed or fruit.

Way seed is spread	How seed or fruit is adapted to the way it is spread
By water	Seed has spines and hooks
By wind	Seed pods dry out and burst open
By animals	Seed has spongy covering that helps it float
By explosion	Seed is very light with thin papery wings

4 Describe another way in which plants are adapted to seed dispersal by animals. Give an example.

_____

_____

_____

_____

5 Why must seeds be spread?

_____

_____

_____

Challenge

Ahmed and Yaseen investigated seed dispersal. They collected three different seeds. They dropped each seed three times and measured how long it stayed in the air each time. These are their results.

Seed	Time in the air Reading 1 (seconds)	Time in the air Reading 2 (seconds)	Time in the air Reading 3 (seconds)	Average time in the air (seconds)
Seed 1 single sycamore	9	10	11	10
Seed 2 dandelion	20	22	24	22
Seed 3 helicopter	15	14	7	12

6   How were the seeds in the investigation dispersed?
Give a reason for your answer.

_____

_____

7   Draw a graph of the average time each seed stayed in the air.

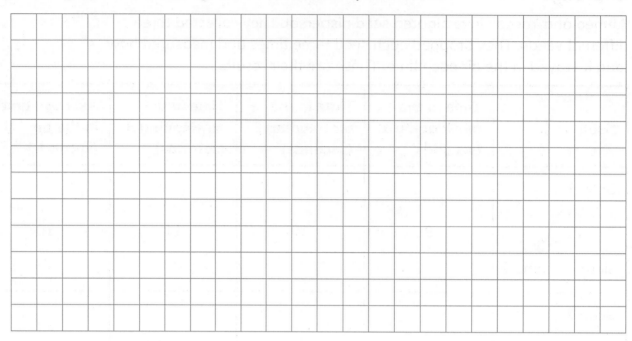

8   a   Which seed stayed in the air longest?

_____

_____

    b   Suggest a reason for this.

_____

9 a   Why did Ahmed and Yaseen repeat their measurements?

   _____

   _____

   b   One result for one of the seeds is quite different to the others.
       Identify the result and suggest a reason for it.

   _____

   _____

10 Say how Ahmed and Yaseen made the investigation a fair test.

   _____

   _____

> 1.4 Seed germination

Focus

1 Match each word about how seeds grow with its description.
   Draw a line from the word to its meaning.

Word		Description	
Germination		The first part that grows
Water		Grows upwards
First root		When a seed starts to grow
First shoot		Makes the seed swell

2   The pictures of the stages of seed germination are in the wrong order.

Number the drawings from 1 to 5 in the correct order.
Then write the number of each drawing in the box next to
its description.

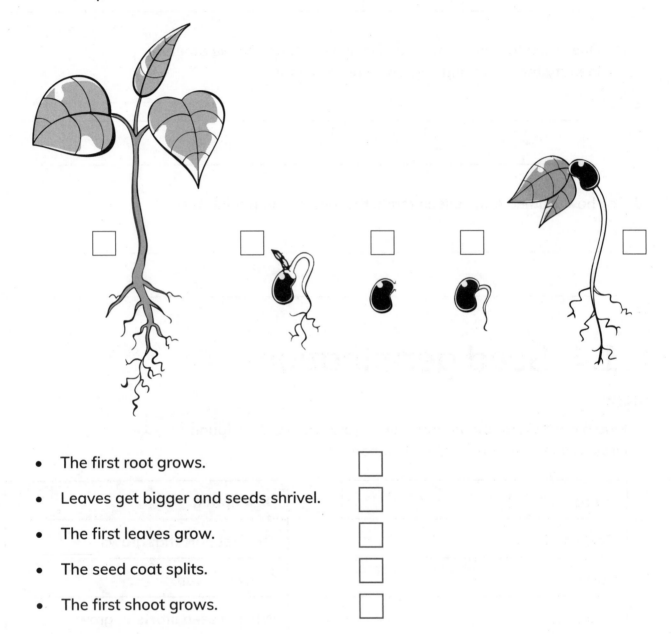

- The first root grows. ☐

- Leaves get bigger and seeds shrivel. ☐

- The first leaves grow. ☐

- The seed coat splits. ☐

- The first shoot grows. ☐

Practice

Class 5 investigated germination. They put seeds on damp cotton wool and placed them into plastic bags. They then put the plastic bags in different places.

They checked the seeds after three days. This is a bar chart of their results.

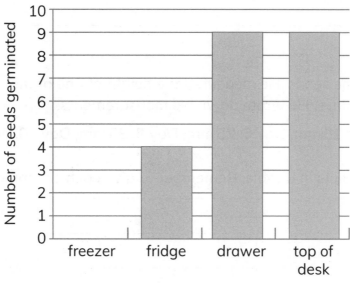

3   In which place did the most seeds germinate?

_____

4   How many seeds germinated in the freezer?

_____

5   Suggest a reason why the same number of seeds germinated in the desk drawer and on the top of the desk.

_____

_____

_____

6   What do the results tell you about the conditions that seeds need to germinate?

_____

_____

_____

Challenge

Arun germinated some seeds. He measured the height of one of the seedlings every two days. He wrote down his measurements:

Day 2: 10 mm, Day 4: 15 mm, Day 6: 25 mm; Day 8: 35 mm, Day 10: 40 mm

7   Present Arun's results in a table. Remember to give each column a heading.

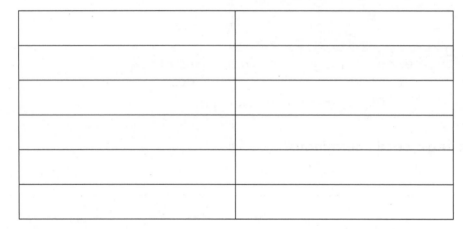

8   Draw a line graph of Arun's results.

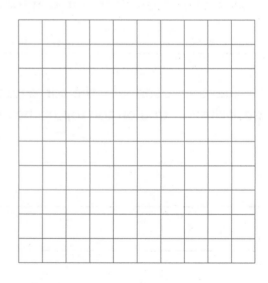

Height of seedling in mm

Time (days)

9 a Where does the seed get the energy it needs for germination?

_____

b Which part of the germinating seed grows first?

_____

c In which direction does it grow?

_____

d Suggest a reason for this.

_____

10 Name two seeds that we eat.

_____

2 Sound

> 2.1 How are sounds made?

Focus

1   Look at the drawing:

a   Complete this drawing to show what will happen if you tap gently
    on the jar with a pencil. You will need to draw in the rice grains.
    Label all parts of the drawing.

b   Complete this drawing to show what will happen if you tap hard on the
    jar with a pencil. Label all the parts of the drawing.

2   Use the words in the box to complete the sentences.

vibrations   more   less   vibrate

a   When you tap the jar it makes the rice grains _____.

b   _____ travel through the jar and plastic wrap to the rice.

c   The rice grains move _____ when you tap the jar gently.

d   The rice grains move _____ when you tap the jar hard.

Practice

Zara and Sofia listened to sounds through different materials.
This is the bar chart they drew to show how loud the sounds were.
Use the bar chart to answer the questions.

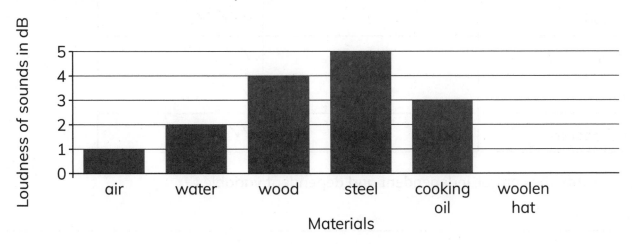

3   Is the material through which the sound was loudest a solid, a liquid or a gas?

_____

4 a Zara and Sofia also listened to sound through a woollen hat.
The loudness of the sound was 3.5dB.
Draw another bar on the bar chart to show this.

b Is wool a solid, a liquid or a gas?

_____

5 Which kinds of materials on the bar chart do sounds travel through best?

_____

Challenge

Zara and Sofia investigated how well sound travels through different materials.
They listened to the sound of a clock ticking through the materials to see
how loud it was. These are their results:

Material	Distance from clock in cm	Loudness of sound
Plastic	0	✓✓✓
Wood	0	✓✓✓✓
Water	2	✓
Air	0	✓
Cardboard	5	✓✓

6 Identify the control, independent and dependent variables.

_____

_____

_____

7 Which material did sound travel through best?

_____

8 Which material(s) did sound travel through worst?

_____

9 Do you think Zara and Sofia's results are accurate? Explain why or why not.

_____

_____

10 What should Zara and Sofia do to get fair and accurate results?

_____

_____

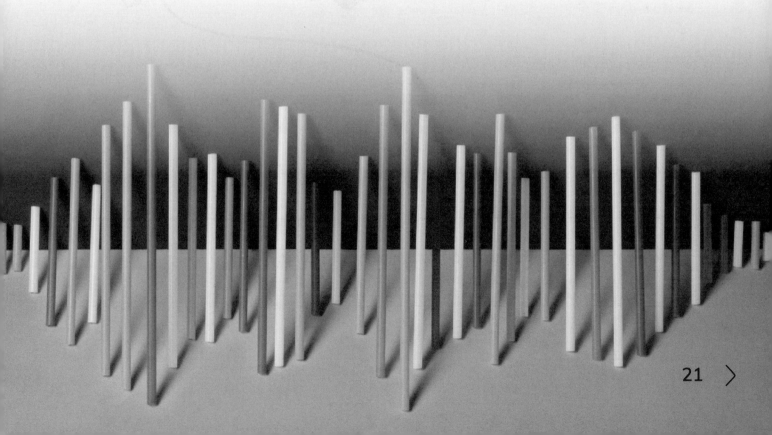

> 2.2 Volume and pitch

Focus

1   Draw a line from each of the sounds shown on the drawings to match its volume.

| 120 | 70 | 100 | 60 | 110 | 0 |

2   What unit is the volume measured in on the drawing?

_____

3   Which of the sounds shown do you think has the highest pitch?

_____

4 How loud do you think a Formula 1 racing car is?
   Is it quieter than, the same as, or louder than the sounds A, B and C below?

A   B   C

A is _____ a formula 1 racing car.

B is _____ a formula 1 racing car.

C is _____ a formula 1 racing car.

Practice

Marcus and his friends used a rating system of ticks to record
the volume of sounds they heard during their lunch break.
These are their results.

Sound	Loudness
Talking	✓✓
Laughing	✓✓✓
Shouting	✓✓✓✓
Music playing	✓✓✓
School bell ringing	✓✓✓✓✓

5   Draw a bar chart of the results. Remember to give your bar chart
    a heading and clearly label the bars and the axes.

6   How could the boys have made more accurate measurements?

_____

7   Identify the control, independent and dependent variables.

_____

_____

_____

8   Which sound was the quietest?

_____

9   How are the vibrations different as a sound gets quieter?

_____

10   Describe how pitch vibrations are different to volume vibrations.

_____

_____

Challenge

Zara and Sofia measured the sound volume of a clock ticking through different materials. These are their results.

Material	Sound in dB
Water	45
Metal	65
Wood	60
Glass	50
Air	40

11 Draw a bar chart of the results.

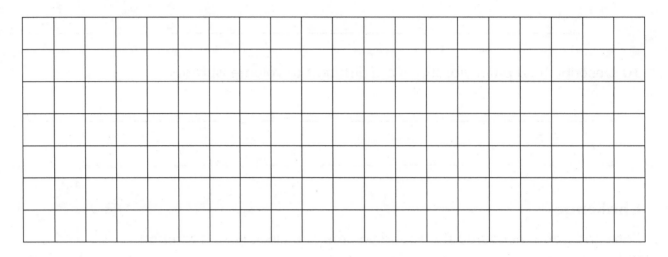

12 a   Which material did sound travel through best?

_____

b   Explain why sound travels well through this material.

_____

13 Identify the control, independent and dependent variables in this investigation.

_____

14 a   Write a conclusion based on the data.

_____

b   How could Zara and Sofia get more evidence to support their conclusion?

_____

> 2.3 Changing the volume of sound

Focus

1   What is volume of sound?

   _____

2   Give an example of a loud sound.

   _____

3   Give an example of a quiet sound.

   _____

4   How does the bell in the picture make a sound?

   _____

   _____

   _____

   _____

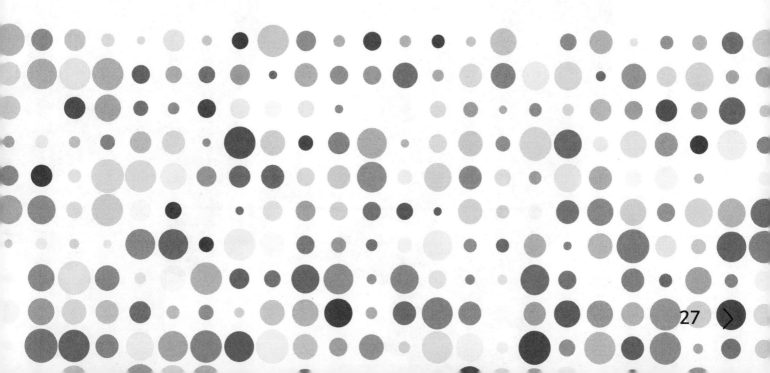

5   Suggest as many ways you can think of to make the sound of the bell ringing louder.
    You can write or draw your ideas.

Practice

6   a   Which material did Zara suggest to muffle the sound of the phone?

    _____

    b   List three other materials that Zara and Sofia could test.

    _____

7   Write down another piece of equipment that they will need to make it
    a fair test besides the materials to test and the mobile phone.

    _____

    _____

8   Name the control variables in their investigation.
    Explain why they are control variables.

    _____

    _____

9   What is the independent variable in their investigation?
    Explain why it is the independent variable.

    _____

    _____

10 What is the dependent variable in their investigation?
    Explain why it is the dependent variable.

    _____

    _____

Challenge

11 Make a drawing to show how Sofia could use a sheet of card to
make sounds louder.

12 Explain how your idea will help Sofia to hear sounds louder.

_____

_____

13 What could you do to improve your design so that it traps more sound
and directs the sound better into her ear?

_____

_____

_____

> 2.4 Changing the pitch of sound

Focus

Look at the picture of Sofia playing the recorder.

1   Complete the sentences about the pitch of the notes Sofia plays.
    Use the words in the box.

> lower   higher   slower   faster   low
>
> longer   shorter   vibrations   high

When Sofia covers fewer air holes with her fingers, it makes the column of air

in the recorder _____ . This makes the air vibrate _____

and gives the sound a _____ pitch.

When Sofia covers more holes with her fingers, it makes the column of air

in the recorder become _____ . This makes the air vibrate

_____ and gives the sound a _____ pitch.

The speed of the air _____ changes the pitch. The pitch can be

_____ or _____ .

Practice

Arun has made a guitar. Look at pictures A, B, C and D of Arun's guitar.
So far he has only put on one string. Suppose Arun presses on the string
at point X and then plucks the string between X and Y.

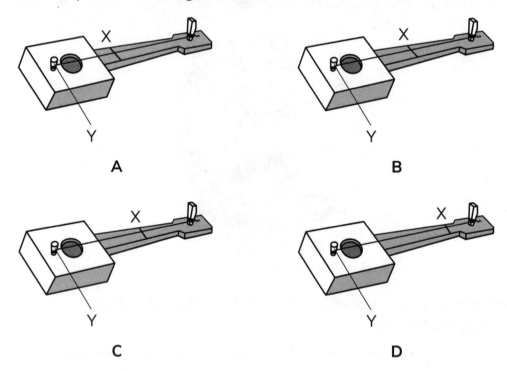

A   B

C   D

2   What is pitch?

_____

3   Will the pitch be highest when the string is plucked between X and Y
    in drawing A, B, C or D? Explain why.

_____

_____

4   How will the pitch of the sound change if the guitar string is thicker?

_____

_____

Challenge

Zara made the musical instrument in the picture.
She filled some bottles with different amounts of water.
To play the instrument Zara blows across the tops of the bottles.

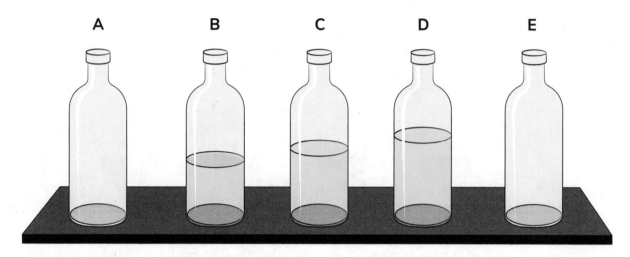

5   What type of musical instrument is this?

_____

6   Which bottle, B, C or D, will produce the sound with the lowest pitch?
    Explain why.

_____

_____

7   Which bottle will produce the sound with the highest pitch? Explain why.

_____

_____

8   Zara wants to put water in the empty bottles A and E.

   a   Draw the level of water she must pour into bottle A to make a lower pitch than B.

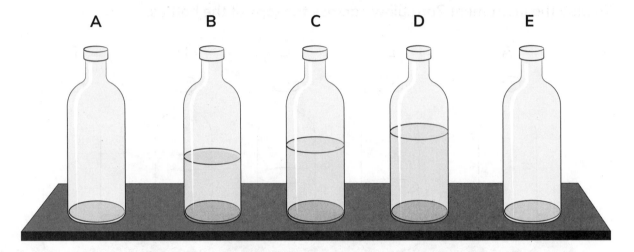

   b   Draw the level of water she must pour into bottle E to make a higher pitch than D.

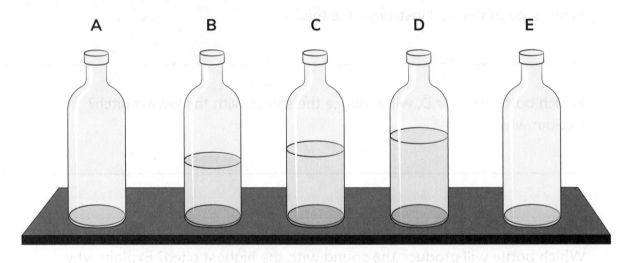

9 Look at the picture of a drum.

How do you think you can change the pitch of the drum?

_____

_____

_____

_____

_____

3 > States and properties of matter

> 3.1 Gases

Focus

Look at the picture of a glass of soda.

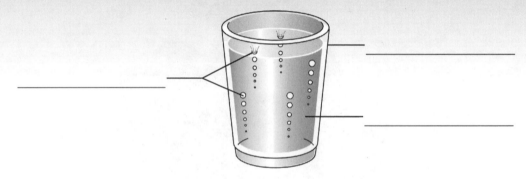

1   Write the labels for solid, liquid and gas in the correct places on the picture.

2   Use the words in the box to complete the sentences about the states of matter.

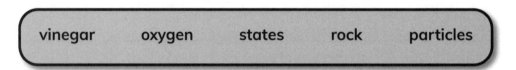

vinegar   oxygen   states   rock   particles

  a   Solids, liquids and gases are the three _____ of matter.

  b   All matter is made of tiny _____.

  c   _____ is an example of a gas.

  d   A _____ is an example of a solid.

  e   _____ is an example of a liquid.

3   Air is a mixture of gases. Say why this is so.

_____

_____

Practice

4   You have 12 particles of matter.
    Draw the 12 particles in each box below to represent a solid, a liquid and a gas.

Solid   Liquid   Gas

5   Fill in the table to describe how particles move in the different states of matter.

State of matter	Do particles move a lot, quite a lot or hardly at all?	Do particles move apart, move far apart or shake in one place?
Solid		
Liquid		
Gas		

Challenge

Look at the pictures of particles in the two syringes, A and B.

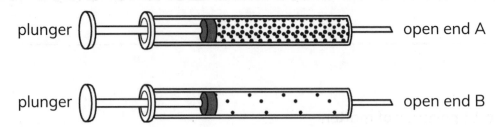

6 a Which syringe do you think contains water and which syringe contains air?

_____

b Explain your answer using the particle model.

_____

_____

_____

_____

7 If you hold your finger over the open end of the syringes, which plunger will be easier to push down? Use the particle model to explain why.

_____

_____

_____

_____

> 3.2 Properties of water

Focus

Choose the correct answer to each of the questions.

Draw a (circle) around the letter of the correct answer to each question.

1 Which process makes ice become liquid on a hot day?

a freezing

b melting

c boiling

d cooling

2 Which answer shows the process of melting?

a liquid + heat ⟶ solid

b gas – heat ⟶ liquid

c solid + heat ⟶ liquid

d solid – heat ⟶ liquid

3 Which answer shows the process of boiling?

a liquid – heat ⟶ gas

b gas + heat ⟶ liquid

c liquid + heat ⟶ gas

d gas – heat ⟶ liquid

4 Which of the following does not happen when we freeze water?

a it solidifies

b it contracts

c it expands

d it changes state

5   Your teacher heats a pan of water. When the water temperature is 100°C, which point has the water reached?

   a   melting point   b   freezing point   c   cooking point   d   boiling point

Practice

Arun put a block of ice on a saucer.

6   Make a drawing to show the ice cube after:

   a   2 minutes   b   10 minutes

7 a What has happened to the ice?

_____

b Why did this process happen?

_____

_____

8 a At what temperature does this process start to happen?

_____

b What do we call this temperature?

_____

Challenge

Sofia's class investigated boiling. These are their results.

Liquid	Temperature at which liquid boils in °C
Pure water	100
Salty water	101
Milk	102
Sugar water	101
Tap water	101

9   What do we call the temperature at which a liquid boils?

_____

10 a   Which liquid boils at the highest temperature?

_____

b   At what temperature does pure water boil?

_____

11 a   Does water always boil at the same temperature? How do you know this?

_____

b   Use the results to suggest a reason for this.

_____

_____

12 Why can't you cook a hard-boiled egg on Mount Everest?
   You may have to do some research find out.

_____

_____

_____

› 3.3 Evaporation and condensation

Focus

1 Underline the correct words to complete these sentences:

Evaporation occurs when a **liquid/gas** changes into a **gas/liquid**. This happens because the particles **gain/lose** heat and move **faster/slower** and **closer together/further apart** until some of them escape from the surface and become a **liquid/gas**.
The opposite process to evaporation is **boiling/condensation**.

2 Decide if the sentences are true or false. Mark each one as either true ✓ or false ✗.

		True	False
a	Evaporation makes wet clothes dry.	☐	☐
b	Water disappears when it evaporates.	☐	☐
c	Condensation occurs when a gas changes to a liquid.	☐	☐
d	Heat makes condensation happen faster.	☐	☐
e	Particles must lose energy before they can condense.	☐	☐

Practice

Zara left some cool drink in a bottle on a windowsill. The next day she opened the bottle and saw that the inside of the lid was wet and there were droplets on the inside of the bottle.

3   What liquid formed inside the lid and on the inside of the bottle?

_____

4   Where did the liquid come from?

_____

5   Name the process that made the liquid form inside the lid.

_____

6   Explain how this process made the liquid form.

_____

_____

_____

7 a   Which process is the reverse of the process you named in question number 5?

_____

   b   Would the drops of liquid have formed without the reverse process?
        Say why or why not.

_____

_____

_____

Challenge

Marcus and Arun investigated the evaporation of water.
They placed two containers of water on the windowsill.

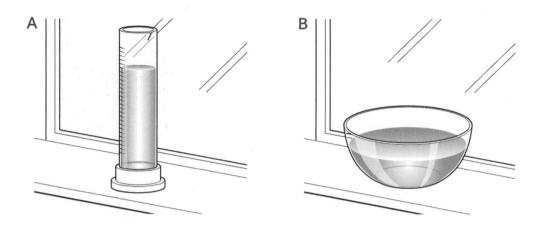

Here are their results.

Day	Volume of water in container in ml	
	Container A	Container B
1	250	250
2	230	200
3	210	160
4	180	120
5	150	80
6		
7		

8   Draw a graph of the results for each container of water.
    Think about the type of graph you should draw.

9   a   From which container did most water evaporate?
        Explain how you know this.

    _____

    _____

    b   Why do you think more water evaporated from that container?

    _____

    _____

10 Predict the results if Marcus and Arun continue their investigation for
    another two days. Fill in your prediction in the table and add the new
    points to your graph.

〉 3.4 Solutions

Focus

1   Arun is writing a report on an investigation. Help him complete his report.
    Use the words in the box to help you.

salt	solute	evaporating
solvent	warm	dissolved
evaporation	solution	
water	evaporated	

Aim

We wanted to find out if you can get salt back from a _____ by

_____ .

Method

We _____ some salt in water in a beaker to make a salt

_____ . The salt was the _____ and the water was

the _____ . We left the beaker in a _____ place for

a few days.

Results

After a few days there was _____ in the bottom of the container.

There was no _____ . It had _____ .

Conclusion

We found that we can get _____ back from a _____ .

We do this by _____ the water.

Practice

Sofia poured hot water into a glass. She added a teaspoon of coffee powder.
She stirred the water.

2　a　Make a drawing of the glass of water and coffee before Sofia stirred it.

　　b　Make a drawing of the glass of water and coffee after Sofia stirred it.

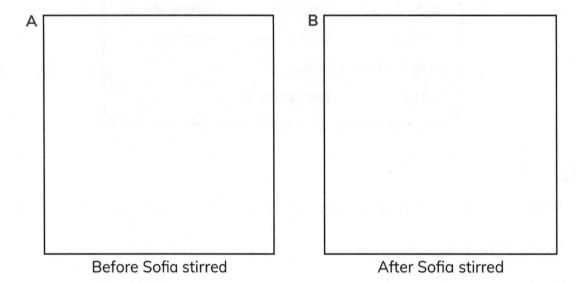

A	B
Before Sofia stirred	After Sofia stirred

　　c　Write the labels 'solute', 'solvent' and 'solution' on your drawings.

3　Explain what happened to the coffee powder when Sofia stirred the water.

_____

_____

_____

4　How can Sofia get the coffee powder back?

_____

_____

_____

Challenge

Marcus put a teaspoonful of sugar into a glass of water to make a solution.
He stirred the mixture. After a while, the sugar disappeared.

5 a Where has the sugar gone?

_____

   b How can you test that the sugar is still there?

_____

   c What part of the solution is the water?

_____

   d What part of the solution is the sugar?

_____

Water and sugar are made up of many tiny particles.
We can represent the particles of water and sugar in a model like this:

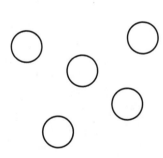

Particles of water

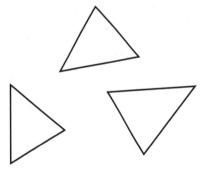

Particles of sugar

6   Use the particle model to draw a picture of the solution Marcus made.
    Label your particles.

7   Marcus added more and more sugar to the solution until no more sugar dissolved.
    Use the particle model to draw a picture of the solution.

4 The digestive system

> 4.1 Parts and functions of the digestive system

Focus

1   Label the diagram of the digestive system. Use these words to help you.

| oesophagus | small intestine | stomach |
| mouth | large intestine | anus |

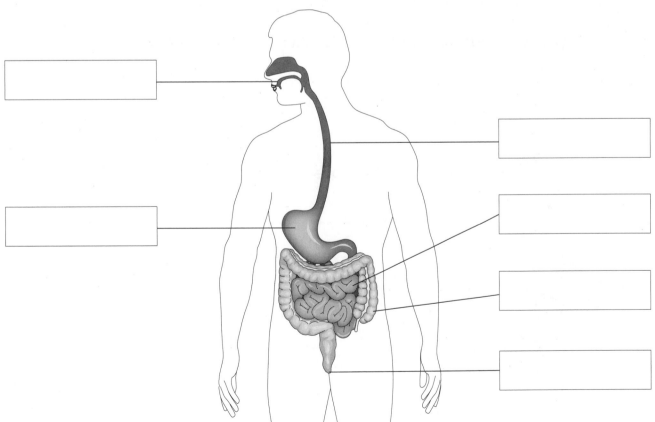

2 a Match each of the labelled parts in question 1 with its function (A–F) listed in the table. Write the name of the part next to its function.

Part	Function
	A Pushes food into the stomach
	B Mixes food with digestive juices
	C Absorbs water and some minerals into the blood
	D Chews food and starts digestion
	E Removes undigested food from the body
	F Breaks food down into very tiny particles

b The functions in the table are not in the same order as they happen in the body. Write the letters of the functions in the correct order.

_____ ⟶ _____ ⟶ _____ ⟶ _____ ⟶ _____ ⟶ _____

Practice

Sofia's group made a model of the human digestive system in the picture.

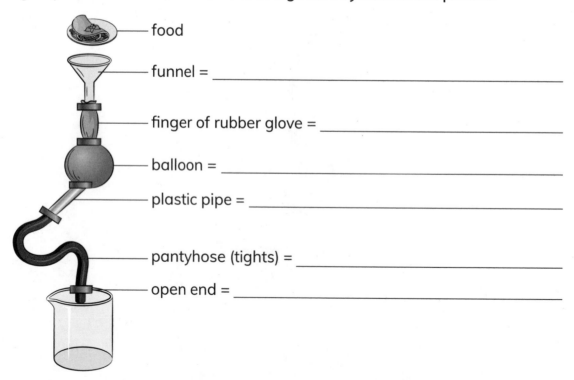

food

funnel = _____

finger of rubber glove = _____

balloon = _____

plastic pipe = _____

pantyhose (tights) = _____

open end = _____

3   Name and label the part of the digestive system that each part of the model represents.

4   How would you change the model to show the digestive system of a squirrel?

_____

_____

Challenge

Class 5 investigated digestion in the mouth.

- They mixed some cooked rice with iodine solution in two beakers.
- They the added 20 ml of saliva to the mixture in one of the beakers.
- They added 20 ml of water to the mixture in the second beaker.
- They observed the two beakers over a period of two hours.

5   Suggest a question that Class 5 was investigating.

_____

6   a   Draw a picture of the two beakers at the start of the investigation.
        Label your picture.

```



```

    b   Explain your drawings.

_____

_____

7   Why did the learners add saliva to one beaker and water to the other beaker?

_____

_____

8   Why did the learners observe the beakers over a period of two hours?

_____

_____

9   a   Draw a picture of the two beakers after two hours.
        Label your picture.

```
┌─────────────────────────────────────────────────────────────┐
│                                                               │
│                                                               │
│                                                               │
│                                                               │
│                                                               │
│                                                               │
│                                                               │
│                                                               │
└─────────────────────────────────────────────────────────────┘
```

    b   Explain your drawings.

    _____

    _____

› 4.2 Balanced diets

Focus

1   Tick (✓) the True or False box for each of these sentences.

	True	False
a A balanced diet gives us all the foods we need to grow and be healthy.	☐	☐
b Proteins build the body.	☐	☐
c We should eat as much sugar as possible to give us energy.	☐	☐
d Vegetables and fruits contain vitamins and minerals our bodies need.	☐	☐

2   Look at the pictures of different foods.

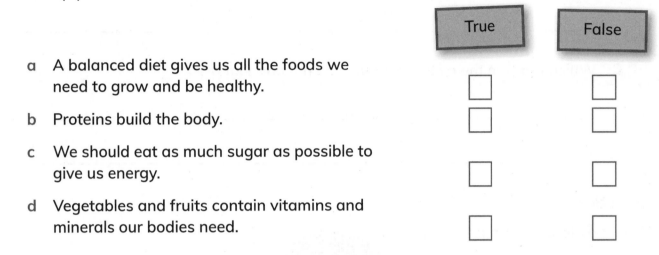

chocolate   eggs   bread   noodles

brown rice   fried chips   tomato   fish

green beans   chicken   watermelon   cookies   cooking oil

a   (Circle) the foods that contain carbohydrates in yellow.

b   (Circle) the foods that contain proteins in red.

c   (Circle) the foods that are fruits and vegetables in green.

d (Circle) the foods that contain mostly fats in black.

e Name two foods in the pictures that contain fibre.

_____

_____

f Which foods in the pictures should you not eat a lot of?

_____

_____

Practice

This is a picture of Arun's lunch.

3 Is his lunch a balanced meal? Say why or why not.

_____

_____

_____

4   a   Suggest a meal for Arun that will be more balanced.
        Draw your meal ideas on the balanced plate and in the glass below.

    b   Label each food group on the plate.

Challenge

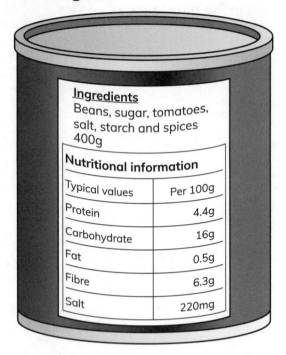

Ingredients
Beans, sugar, tomatoes, salt, starch and spices
400g

Nutritional information	
Typical values	Per 100g
Protein	4.4g
Carbohydrate	16g
Fat	0.5g
Fibre	6.3g
Salt	220mg

Beans with tomato sauce

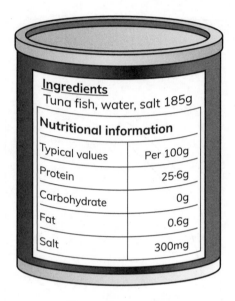

Ingredients
Tuna fish, water, salt 185g

Nutritional information	
Typical values	Per 100g
Protein	25·6g
Carbohydrate	0g
Fat	0.6g
Salt	300mg

Tuna in water

5   List the different food groups found in the can of beans.

_____

_____

6   Explain why you need to eat foods containing proteins.

_____

_____

7   Budi ate 100 g of beans.

　　a   How much protein did he eat?

　　_____

b　How much carbohydrates did the beans contain?

_____

c　Budi's big brother ate a whole can of beans.
　　How much carbohydrates did he eat?

_____

8 a　Which can contains the most protein per 100 g?

_____

b　Which food contains the most salt?

_____

9 a　Which of the foods would it be best for Budi to eat before he plays
　　a game of football? Say why.

_____

_____

b　Which food is best for building new cells in the body? Say why.

_____

_____

c　Which food is best for helping food move easily through the digestive system?
　　Say why.

_____

_____

5 ▶ Forces and magnetism

> 5.1 Gravity, normal forces and applied forces

Focus

1   What type of diagram is this?

    _____

2   Name force A.

    _____

3   Is force A a pulling force or a pushing force?

    _____

4   Name force B.

    _____

5   Is force B a pulling force or a pushing force?

_____

6   Look at the picture.

     Complete these sentences about the picture:

     Marcus _____ the cricket ball.

     This is an _____ force.

Practice

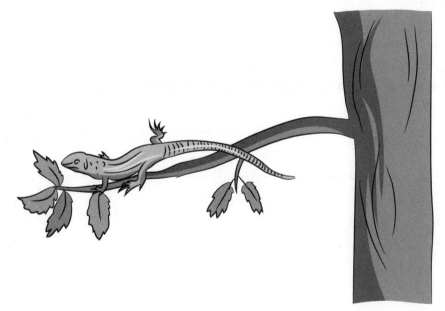

7   a   Make this drawing into a force diagram.
          Draw the two forces acting on the lizard.

     b   Show the directions that the forces are working in.

     c   Label each force.

8 A

B

a   Which picture, A or B, shows a pulling force?

_____

b   Which picture, A or B, shows a pushing force?

_____

c   Explain why both pictures show an applied force.

_____

_____

Challenge

9 Draw a force diagram to show the two forces acting on a box on a table.

Remember to:

- draw arrows to show the direction the forces are acting
- label the forces.

10 In each of the following pictures A and B:

a describe what the person is doing

b identify the force as a push or a pull force, or both

c explain why it is an applied force.

A

B

Picture A

a _____

b _____

c _____

Picture B

a _____

b _____

c _____

> 5.2 Gravity and satellites

Focus

Answer questions 1–4 by completing the sentences.

1 What is a satellite?

   A satellite is a body which orbits a _____ body in space.

2 What type of satellite is the Moon?

   The Moon is a _____ satellite of the Earth.

3 What type of satellite is a communications satellite?

   A communications satellite is an _____ satellite.

4 What force of attraction exists between the Earth and the Moon?

   The Moon and the Earth are attracted towards each other by the force

   of _____ .

5   Look at the diagram.

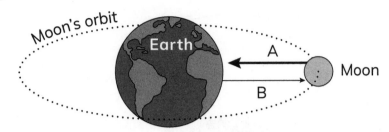

a   Which force line, A or B, shows the force of gravity that the Earth exerts on the Moon?

_____

b   Why is A a thicker arrow than B?

_____

_____

Practice

6   a   What is a natural satellite?

_____

b   Give an example.

_____

7   a   What is an artificial satellite?

_____

b   Give an example.

_____

8 Complete the diagram of an artificial satellite orbiting the Earth.

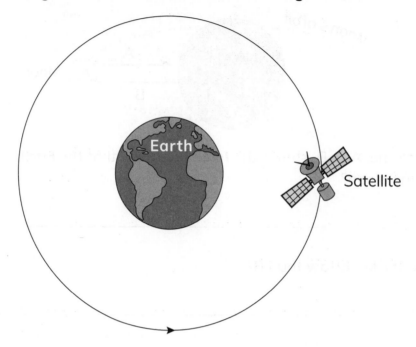

a   Draw a force arrow to represent the force of gravity between the Earth and the satellite.

b   Draw a force arrow to represent the force of gravity between the satellite and the Earth.

9 Explain why you drew one arrow thicker than the other.

_____

_____

_____

_____

_____

_____

Challenge

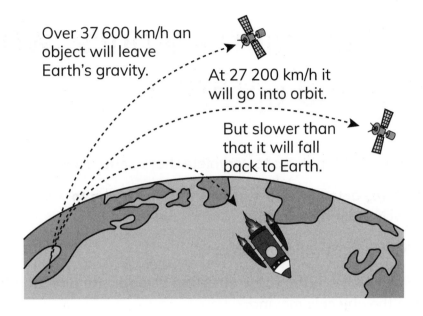

Over 37 600 km/h an object will leave Earth's gravity.

At 27 200 km/h it will go into orbit.

But slower than that it will fall back to Earth.

10 What type of satellite is shown on the diagram?

_____

11 What launches the satellite into space?

_____

12 Why is it necessary for the satellite to travel at over 37 600 km/h when it leaves the surface of the Earth?

_____

13 When the satellite travels at 27 200 km/h, what path does it follow?

_____

14 What force keeps the satellite following this path?

_____

15 What happens to the satellite if its speed drops below 27 200 km/h?

_____

> 5.3 Friction, air resistance, water resistance and upthrust

Focus

1   Underline the correct alternatives to complete these sentences.

   a   Friction is a force between two surfaces that are trying to **slide past each other/remain still**.

   b   Friction only acts on **still/moving** objects.

   c   Friction always works in the **same direction as/opposite direction from** the direction the object is moving.

   d   Friction **speeds up/slows down** the moving object.

   e   Water resistance **slows things down/speeds things up** that are moving through water.

   f   Air resistance **slows things down/speeds things up** that are moving through air.

   g   Look at the picture of the log in the water.

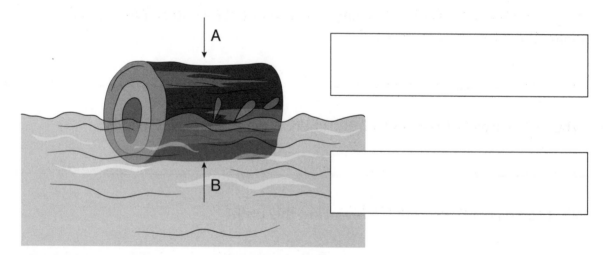

Label the two forces, A and B, acting on the log.

Practice

The drawing shows two people jumping with parachutes.

A

B

2 a Which parachute, A or B, will fall faster?

_____

b Explain why.

_____

_____

3 On the drawing, draw and label the forces acting on the parachutes.
Show the direction in which each force acts.

4   a   Do you think the parachutes fall faster or slower when the person is heavier?

_____

    b   Explain why.

_____

_____

    c   How could you test this idea?

_____

_____

_____

Challenge

5   Look at the picture of a dolphin.

A dolphin can move very fast through the sea. Give two reasons why it can do this.

_____

_____

6   Look at the picture of a lorry.

Lorries travel for long distances on motorways.

a   Which force slows down these lorries because of their size?

_____

b   How do you think the design feature marked by the arrow helps the lorry
     to travel faster?

_____

_____

c   How do you think the design feature marked by the arrow helps the lorry
     to save fuel?

_____

_____

› 5.4 Multiple forces

Focus

1   Draw a (circle) around the correct answer for questions a–c.

   a   Force A is:

   • Gravity   • Normal force   • Friction

   b   Force B is:

   • Gravity   • Normal force   • Friction

   c   Force C is:

   • Gravity   • Normal force   • Friction

2   Name another force that will slow Arun down on a windy day.

   _____

3   What must Arun do to overcome the force you named in Question 2?

   _____

Practice

4 On the diagram, label the four forces that act on an aeroplane when it is flying.

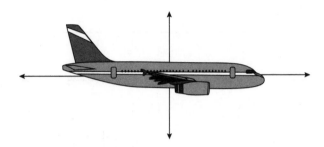

5 Which two forces are natural forces?

_____

6 Which two forces are provided by the aeroplane?

_____

7 People got their ideas from birds flying when they designed aeroplanes.
  Look at the drawing below. Label the forces.

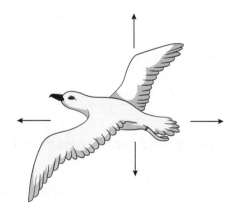

8   Which forces are natural forces?

_____

9   How does the bird overcome these forces to be able to fly?

_____

_____

Challenge

Look at the picture of the person swimming.

10 Draw and label the four forces acting on the swimmer.

11 Name the three natural forces.

_____

_____

_____

12 What does the swimmer have to do to overcome these forces and move forward?

_____

13 How do swimmers make themselves more streamlined?

_____

_____

> 5.5 Magnets and magnetic materials

Focus

1   Tick (✓) 'Yes' if the object is made of magnetic material.

Tick (✓) 'No' if the object is made from non-magnetic material.

cast iron pot	rubber gloves	wooden spoon	wool
☐ Yes ☐ No	☐ Yes ☐ No	☐ Yes ☐ No	☐ Yes ☐ No
steel paperclip	plastic bottle	aluminium pot	gold rings
☐ Yes ☐ No	☐ Yes ☐ No	☐ Yes ☐ No	☐ Yes ☐ No
rubber tyre	plastic bucket	brass candlestick	iron nails
☐ Yes ☐ No	☐ Yes ☐ No	☐ Yes ☐ No	☐ Yes ☐ No

Practice

2   Your grandma drops a box of pins on the floor.

    a   Describe how you could help her pick the pins up easily using a magnet.

    _____

    _____

    b   Why does the magnet pick up the pins?

    _____

    _____

3   There is a mixture of iron nails and wood shavings on the floor of the workshop.

    a   How can you get the nails out using a magnet?

    _____

    _____

    b   Why does the magnet pick up the nails?

    _____

    _____

    c   Why doesn't the magnet pick up the wood shavings?

    _____

    _____

Challenge

A compass has a magnetic pointer or needle that is attracted to the Earth's magnetic north pole.

Zara and Sofia decided to make a simple compass. They used a polystyrene cup and some water, a cork, a sheet of A4 paper and a pen, a bar magnet, a large steel needle, a small piece of sticky tape and some steel pins. Here are the steps they took to make the compass:

- They wrote the points of the compass ('N' for north, 'S' for south, 'E' for east and 'W' for west) at the edges of the A4 paper.
  They placed the paper on a flat surface far away from any metal objects.
- They put a little water in the cup. They placed the cup in the middle of the paper.
- They stuck the needle to the table with a small piece of sticky tape.
- They stroked the needle with one pole of the bar magnet. They stroked in the same direction and made sure the bar magnet was well clear of the needle at the end of each stroke.
- They continued stroking for about 5 minutes. Then they tested to see if the needle was magnetic by trying to pick up paper clips with it.
- They pushed the needle through the cork and floated it in the water in the cup.
- They turned the cup until the needle was lined up north–south on the paper. The needle stayed pointing north because it was attracted to the Earth's north pole.

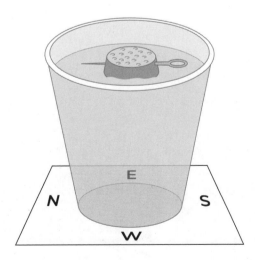

4 Why did they use a steel needle to make the compass?

_____

5 Why did they stroke the needle with a magnet?

_____

6 Why did they test the needle by trying to pick up paper clips with it?

_____

7 Why did they use a cork to stick the needle through?

_____

8 Why did they use a polystyrene cup for the water?

_____

9 Why did they put the compass far from any metal objects?

_____

> 5.6 Magnetic force

Focus

Arun and Marcus had two bar magnets. They did an investigation to find out which magnet was strongest. They used a plastic ruler and a metal paper clip to compare the distance from which the magnets attract the paper clip.

Here is a table of their results:

Magnet	Distance in mm – first reading	Distance in mm – second reading	Distance in mm – third reading	Average (mean) reading in mm
Magnet 1 – N. pole	35	28	30	
Magnet 1 – S. pole	31	26	27	
Magnet 2 – N. pole	51	46	53	
Magnet 2 – S. pole	54	49	52	

1 Complete the table by filling in the average (mean) readings.

2 Why did they make three readings for each pole of each magnet?

_____

3 Why did they use a metal paper clip and not a plastic-coated paper clip?

_____

_____

4 Which magnet was the strongest, Magnet 1 or Magnet 2?

_____

5 Which pole of the strongest magnet was strongest, the north or the south pole?

_____

6 What conclusion did Arun and Marcus make about the strength of magnets?

_____

_____

Practice

Marcus compares the strength of two bar magnets (A and B).
He has three pieces of card 10 × 10 cm and a steel screw.

This is what Marcus does:

- Step 1: Marcus places the screw on a
  table underneath one piece of card.
  He holds magnet A over the card. The
  screw sticks to the magnet through
  the card, so he can pick up the card
  and screw with the magnet.
- He repeats Step 1 with Magnet B and
  gets the same result.

- Step 2: he now puts two pieces of card between the magnet and the screw. The screw still sticks to the magnet through two pieces of card when he uses magnet A and magnet B.
- Step 3: he now puts three pieces of card between the magnet and the screw. The screw still sticks to the magnet through three pieces of card when he uses magnet A. But when he uses magnet B the screw does not stick to the cards.

7   Why does the screw stick to the magnet through the card when Marcus holds the magnet over the card?

_____

_____

8   Which magnet was strongest, A or B? Explain why.

_____

_____

9   List two ways that Marcus's experiment was a fair test.

_____

_____

10 Could Marcus have used a cork or a plastic button instead of a screw to test the strength of the magnets? Explain why or why not.

_____

_____

Challenge

Maglev stands for 'magnetic levitation'. 'Levitation' means floating above the ground. Magnets on the track push and lift the train up in the air by 3 to 15 cm. So a maglev train floats above the tracks on a 'cushion' of magnetic force. The magnets in the track are extremely strong and very expensive.

If a country wants to use a maglev train they have to build a completely new magnetic track. It is not possible to change an old train track into a maglev train track.

Maglev trains float on air. This means there is no friction with a track. This lack of friction allows these trains to reach speeds of more than 500 kilometres per hour.

Maglev trains have no wheels. This makes them quieter than normal trains.

Maglev trains use 30% less energy than normal trains.

11 What are Maglev train tracks made of?

_____

12 What keeps a Maglev train moving 3 to 15 cm above the track?

_____

13 Give three advantages of the Maglev train compared to a train that runs
on metal tracks.

_____

_____

_____

14 What is the main disadvantage of the Maglev train?

_____

_____

_____

_____

15 Find out which countries use Maglev trains.

_____

_____

_____

_____

_____

6 ▶ Seasons and adaptations of plants and animals

> 6.1 The Earth moves around the Sun

Focus

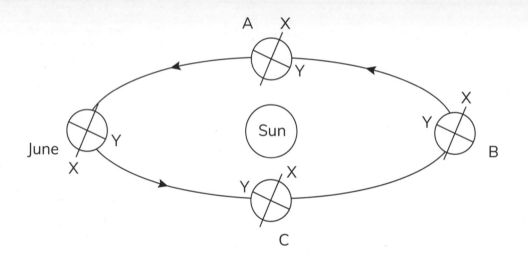

1   What shape is the Earth's orbit around the Sun?

   _____

2   In which direction does the Earth orbit the Sun?

   _____

3   What is the imaginary line labelled X?

   _____

4 What is the imaginary line labelled Y?

_____

5 How long does it take Earth to complete its orbit around the Sun?

_____

6 Find the position of Earth labeled June.
   Which month will Earth be at when it reaches the following points?

   C _____

   B _____

   A _____

7 What is the length of day and night all over the world in positions A and C?

_____

Practice

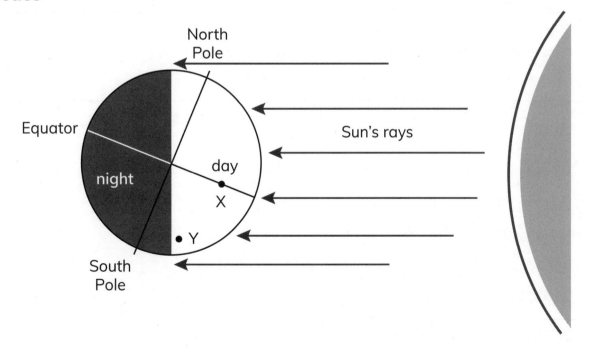

8   a   Which hemisphere is having summer?

_____

    b   Explain your answer.

_____

9   a   What will the length of day be at X?

_____

    b   What time will sunrise and sunset be at X?

_____

10 a   If you lived at Y would you need to wear a thick coat outside?

_____

    b   Explain why or why not.

_____

11 Which month of the year does this diagram represent?

_____

Challenge

The diagram shows the Earth in four positions during its orbit around the Sun.

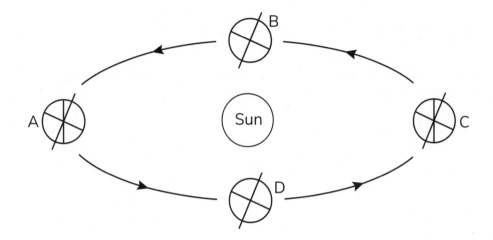

12 How long does it take the Earth to complete one orbit around the Sun?

_____

13 On the diagram, colour in the area having night on each Earth.

14 a In position A, what season are people experiencing in the northern hemisphere?

_____

b Explain how you know this.

_____

15 a In position C, what season are people experiencing in the northern hemisphere?

_____

b Explain how you know this.

_____

16 What is the length of day and night everywhere on Earth in positions B and D?

_____

17 On the diagram, label the month that each Earth represents.

18 For how many days of the year will the Earth occupy the positions shown on the diagram? Explain your answer.

_____

_____

› 6.2 Seasonal changes

Focus

Here is some data about sunrise and sunset in Karachi, Pakistan.

Date	Sunrise	Sunset	Length of day	Change – is day getting longer or shorter?
March 16th	06:40	18:41	12 h 01 min	–
+ 1 day	06:39	18:42		
+1 week	06:33	18:44		
+2 weeks	06:26	18:47		
+1 month	06:10	18:54		
+2 months	05:48	19:09		
+3 months	05:42	19:22		
+6 months	06:18	18:37		

1 Complete the table by filling in the length of day column.
   Then write 'longer' or 'shorter' for each line with a + sign in the last column.

2 Identify the pattern shown by the data for the length of day between
   March and June.

   _____

3 a Is Karachi going from spring to summer or from autumn to winter
      between March and June?

      _____

   b Explain how you know this.

      _____

4 Explain the data in the +6 months line.

   _____

5 What is the difference between animal migration and hibernation?

   _____

   _____

Practice

The graph shows the sunrise and sunset times for Doha, Qatar.

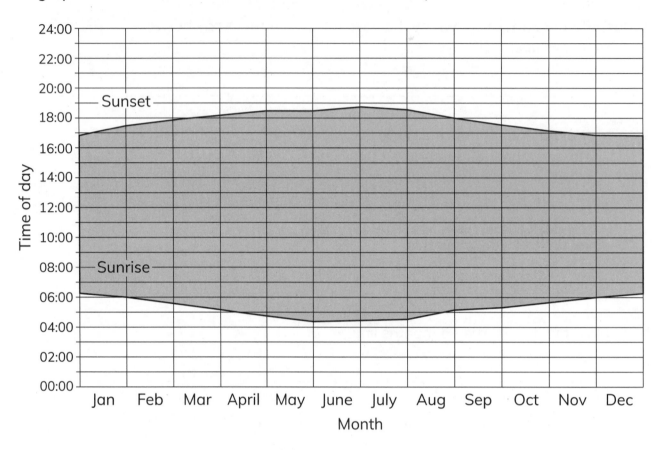

Answer these questions about the graph.

6   What causes sunrise and sunset?

_____

7   What does the height of any shaded part of the graph represent?

_____

8   What pattern does the graph show between January and June?

_____

9 In which months do you think Doha has summer?

_____

10 What causes the pattern shown on the graph?

_____

Challenge

Arctic terns

Arctic terns are sea birds which fly about 40 000 km each year. That's about equal to the distance around the Earth. These birds experience summer in the Arctic and summer in the Antarctic.

Chicks hatch in Greenland in the summer. In September the parents and the young birds fly all the way to the Antarctic to feed during the Antarctic summer. They feed on small fish in the Weddell Sea. In April they return to the Arctic.

An Arctic tern can live for 25 years. During its life it can fly a million kilometres – nearly three times the distance from the Earth to the Moon.

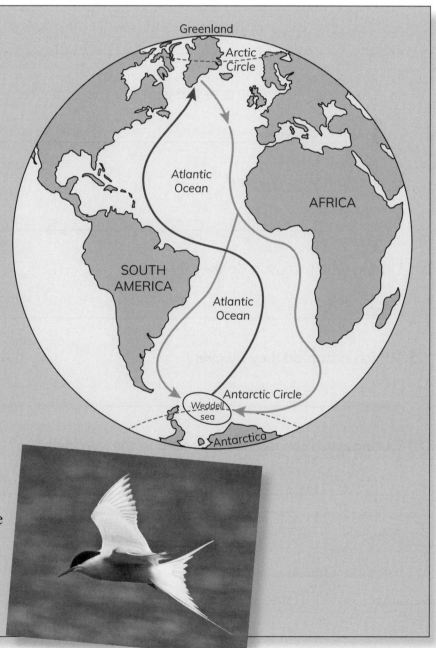

Use the map and the story and your knowledge from the topic to find the answers to the following questions.

11 Does the Arctic tern migrate or hibernate?

_____

12 Give two reasons why the birds do this.

_____

_____

13 a During which months of the year are the Arctic terns in Greenland?

_____

b Explain your answer

_____

14 During which season do they fly south?

_____

15 Which ocean do they fly over?

_____

16 During which season do they feed in the Weddell Sea?

_____

> 6.3 Plants and animals are adapted to different environments

Focus

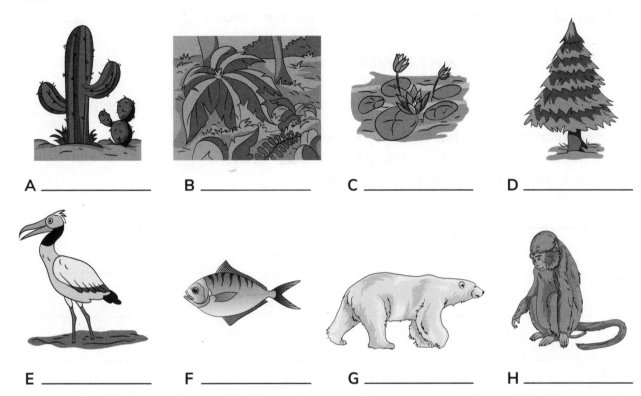

A _____ B _____ C _____ D _____

E _____ F _____ G _____ H _____

1   Identify each plant **A–D**. Choose from water lily, tropical plant, cactus and fir tree.

For each plant say what type of environment it is adapted to.
Use the words 'hot', 'cold', 'wet' and 'dry' in your answers
(some answers need more than one word).

A _____

B _____

C _____

D _____

2 Match one of the following adaptations numbered 1–4 to each plant **A–D**.

    1 Large leaves that can lose water. _____

    2 Large flat leaves that float on water. _____

    3 Needles instead of leaves that do not lose much water. _____

    4 Thorns instead of leaves which lose very little water. _____

3 Identify each animal **E–H**. Choose from polar bear, fish, wading bird, monkey.

    For each animal say what type of environment it is adapted to.
Use the words 'hot', 'cold', 'wet' and 'dry' in your answers
(some answers need more than one word).

    E _____

    F _____

    G _____

    H _____

4 Match one of the following adaptations numbered 1–4 to each animal **E–H**.

    1 Long arms and legs to climb up trees and swing on branches to get

       food in forest. _____

    2 Long legs to wade in water. _____

    3 Thick layer of fat and fur to keep warm. _____

    4 Gills to get oxygen from water. _____

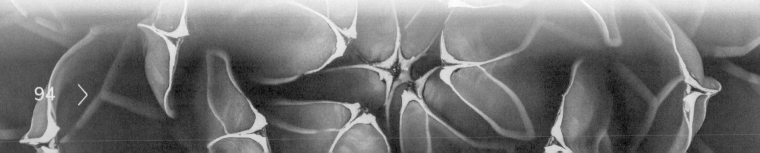

Practice

This picture is of an emperor penguin.
This animal lives in Antarctica which is very cold and full of ice and snow.

Emperor penguins hunt for fish in the sea. The female lays one egg.
The male keeps the egg warm while the female hunts for food.

Read about the adaptations this animal has to survive in such a cold,
icy environment.

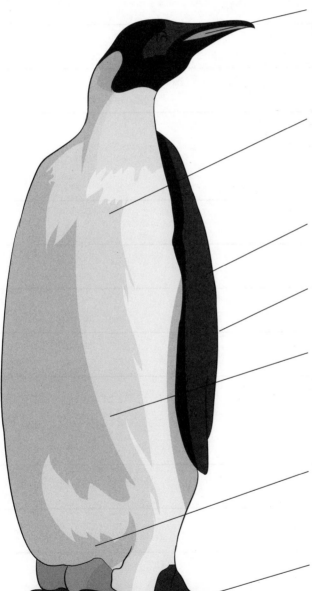

The penguin's nostrils take in heat when the penguin breathes out. This warms up the icy air that the penguin breathes in.

Three layers of feathers to keep body warm. The feathers are oily so that the penguin stays dry while it is on land.

Flippers for swimming.

Streamlined body shape for swimming fast.

Layer of fat under the skin to keep warm and to feed off in the weeks the penguin does not eat while he is looking after the egg.

Special fold of skin to cover egg which rests on its feet.

Feet are standing on the ice. They have good blood supply to keep warm. Feet are also strong and help penguin to swim fast and catch fish.

5 Make a list of the adaptations an emperor penguin has to survive in a cold, icy environment. Use the headings below.

Keeping warm

_____

_____

_____

_____

_____

Getting food

_____

_____

_____

_____

_____

Looking after the egg

_____

_____

_____

_____

_____

Challenge

Adaptations of frogs

Frogs have many adaptations that allow them to live either in a wet environment or a dry environment.

Frogs may breathe through their skin or use their lungs. When they are in water, oxygen from the water is dissolved into the frog's thin skin. From there the oxygen passes through the walls Frogs have many adaptations that allow them to live either in a wet environment or a dry environment.

Frogs may breathe through their skin or use their lungs. When they are in water, oxygen from the water is dissolved into the frog's thin skin. From there the oxygen passes through the walls of the blood vessels into the blood. When on land, frogs are able to breathe through their lungs at the same time as with their skin. The lungs are a much more efficient way for frogs to get oxygen. Frogs can close their noses to prevent taking in water into their lungs when they are swimming.

A frog's skin is covered with a slimy substance called mucus. The mucus stops its skin from drying out. Frogs replace their skin weekly by pulling off old skin to reveal new skin underneath. A new skin every week makes sure that their skin stays soft and coated with the protective mucus.

Frogs have webbed feet that allow them to move through the water more efficiently. Their strong hind legs help them to swim and leap better when they are on land.

They can see very well even in muddy water and in the dark.

6 Use the information in this case study about frogs to complete this table.

Part of frog	Adaptation in water	Adaptation on land
Breathing		
Nose		
Skin		
Legs and feet		
Eyesight		

> 6.4 Adaptations of predators and prey

Focus

1   Identify three predators and three prey in these pictures.
    Match each predator with its prey.

    _____

    _____

    _____

2   For each predator, give two adaptations it has that make it a successful predator.

    _____

    _____

    _____

3 For each prey, give two adaptations it has that help it to avoid being eaten by its predator.

_____

_____

_____

Practice

Owls live in trees. They are predators that hunt at night.

Large eyes that can see in the dark are set in front of their face

Sharp, hooked beak

Can move neck in almost a complete circle

Fringed feathers on wings muffle sound

Patterned brown and grey colours

Sharp claws

4   List seven adaptations of owls.
    Describe how each adaptation makes owls very successful night predators.

    _____

    _____

    _____

    _____

    _____

    _____

5   Use secondary sources, such as the internet or library books, to list examples
    of the prey that owls hunt.

    _____

    _____

    _____

6   Suggest adaptations which the prey has in order to avoid being caught
    by an owl.

    _____

    _____

    _____

Challenge

Choose a predator and its prey that lives in your country.
Do some research to find the answers to these questions.

7   Name the predator and prey.

_____

8   Describe the environment in which the predator and prey live.

_____

9   Describe the adaptations of the predator.

_____

_____

_____

_____

10 Describe the adaptations of the prey.

_____

_____

_____

_____

Acknowledgements

The authors and publishers acknowledge the following sources of copyright material and are grateful for the permissions granted. While every effort has been made, it has not always been possible to identify the sources of all the material used, or to trace all copyright holders. If any omissions are brought to our notice, we will be happy to include the appropriate acknowledgements on reprinting.

Thanks to Getty Images for permission to reproduce images.

Cover by Pablo Gallego(Beehive Illustration); *Inside* **Unit 1** Ed Reschke/GI; mammuth/GI; ullstein bild/GI; Lisa Romerein/GI; ©Daniela White Images/GI; Neil Holmes/GI; Mike Powles/GI; Paul Starosta/GI; Barbara Rich/GI; **Unit 2** MirageC/GI; Jobalou/GI; Peter Dazeley/GI; Frank Ramspott/GI; **Unit 3** Jose A. Bernat Bacete/GI; Unit 5 Jeff Mccollough/GI; pidjoe/GI; **Unit 6** Matt_Gibson/GI; Feng Wei Photography/ GI; Alexander Spatari/GI; ithinksky/GI; Jonas's Photo/GI; David Rius & Núria Tuca/GI; zahoor salmi/GI; Adam Jones/GI; Alastair Pollock Photography/GI; Robert Smits/GI

Key GI=Getty Images